The five stages of my mood

Sonia Sandru

BookLeaf
Publishing
India | USA | UK

Presentation by *BookLeaf Publishing*

Web: www.bookleafpub.com

E-mail: info@bookleafpub.com

ISBN : 9789357448123

First edition 2021

Morning in blue

The moon is still up on the night sky.
It's almost morning, and yet, here I am.
Still awake,
maybe I am dreaming and yet I cannot stop.
I look out the window,
It is still dark, yet it's morning.
I do not understand
But I do know that I cannot stop.
Maybe tomorrow, or by the light of dawn
Or the first ray of morning light.

Island of time

Island of dream,
Empire of eternal sorrow and the voiceless
souls,
Oh, lake of fire, that swallows every breath,
Not life nor death is left,
In time and in dream, I wander through your
land,
There's no end and no destiny,
No escape and no fate.

Storm at sea

There is so much noise.
I sit here on a chair,
I look at a white building with golden tops and
one strange poise.
I stare at the sea, a strange colour of mixed
turquoise and blue.
It wasn't so the last time I was here.
It was three layers of dark green and blue
and the horizon seemed so far and so
mysterious.
Why is it that today, it looks so close and so
unappealing?
This sand filled green, makes me think,
Was there a storm at sea?
In the great vastness of the sea,
did the winds and the gods beneath fight all
night?
or was Neptune just in a bad mood?
This wind and this weather,
make my scars feel soft and tender.
As if I was back in those times, about 60 months
before.
I looked at it early in this morning,
It was so pink on pale skin.
The Sun today, it makes children laugh

and so, they brave the sea and its cold stones,
yet here I am, sitting on a chair, so close to a shiver
and I hold in hand a small paper river.

Storm

The sky is crying.
The light is here but darkness covers from high
above
And they all intertwine.
The sky and the Heavens are filled with sorrow
And it snows upon green hills.
They were beautiful and now there is none
They were filled with joy and now there's
sorrow.
Tears fall and the skies abide
There was light and there was colour.
There was water and there was the Sun.
May the Light be everlasting,
May the Night be unchanged
Together may they be unbound
And so, there is life.

Cold wine

How time flies.
The New Year is again upon us.
And yet here I sit, alone.
Snowflakes fall down from up above,
Remiss of fate.
And here you are!
Bringing food and warm wine.
Don't you know?
You are giving warm wine to the cursed man.
You are giving wine, to a man of broken heart.

How time flies!
The New Year is upon us again.
And yet here you sit, alone.
Snowflakes rise above from down below.
Shackled by the fate.
Here I am!
Bringing food and cold wine.
Do I know?
I bring food and cold wine to a silent man.
I give wine to the one whose heart is cold.
Wine to a man whose lost and frozen in time.

Don't we know?

We come to those who were.
Now there's only ghosts, solitude and wine.

Still night

it is the night of the cold wind,
I drink and then I think.
how many more should I still feel.
I thought a decade could be
a light breeze brings to me
a dry old leaf from a dark fir tree.

Sky dance

I travel through the long stone paths
Up to the mountain sides.
The sky should be dark,
It is twelve at night.
There is no clock so there is no one,
But there's a thunder and a light,
I watch high up in the sky.
There's no clouds and it's so bright,
I want to dance but one night.
There's lighting and there's a drum,
Beg the havens for a chance
Let me see how they dance.
There's the strike and then on twice,
 I become one with the purple skies.

September's end

It all doesn't make much sense,
I wait and to no end.
Summer's gone and now September ends,
leaves turn red and green is gone
The winds are rising even more,
I turn left, green sea,
I turn right, sapphire sky.
There's a pair of sand like shoes,
I step on one and I fall twice,
I step on two and I move, too.

October 6

Today everything is irritating,
all my stories are annoying.
Not my songs and not my poems
Are all that heroic.
All I want is but one rime,
there's an apple on my table,
four lights and a candle.
There's an incense and a kettle.
I watch the smoke and I turn twice.
I sit down and hold my pen.
'tis past twelve, I still write,
I want a poem or a song
There's none that I can recall,
How'd I write all this by now?
I say it is alright,
All I need is one more line.

At the window

I have a portrait and a poet,
it is hot and I must not.
Three numbers I recall,
I have a hunger that cannot stop,
I should run so I forward.
There's a beauty at the window,
I stay low so that I can below.
There's a song that I recall
Never had I been told what in winter I can
behold.

Mist

My sweet, sweet, beloved mist.
Every day I long for you
and every day it is in vain.
by Monday it is too late,
by today 'tis not our fate.
It was a week and then three,
Now there's more than I can count,
but still you are not to be found.

Orange blossom

There's an orange sapling in my town
That's never in bloom when ones around.
It's fragrant little flowers to be witnessed but by
the moon.
Only once a year we all see,
the beauty of this tree.
When it's time for it to bear fruit,
We can all enjoy the light orange view.

Wisteria of downtown

There's a house downtown,
 By the old mill ridge,
And there's a wisteria tree so proud.
It's a guardian for all we know,
it stands tall and bright, by the candlelight.
It's been there for two whole ages now.
Changed its owner twice every six decades past.
Every summer there's a purple mist.
The blooms fly all night,
everywhere in the town at night.
There's no spirits and no haunting,
So long as there's a wisteria so beloved.
But then one day, there was a woman dressed in
blue.
Her soft voice spoke to the small new buds
The tree is so at peace,
and it blooms all to bid her will.
But then a half age is gone.
"Where is she?" and she is not.
She won't be back, and the tree won't bloom,
Where's the master? He is gone.

There's another half age past and a sadness to
last.
The wisteria, it is so sad,
There is no more bloom, and it won't stay,
Already it shines much less.
Soon the village will be plagued by and endless
swarm of ghosts.
Now the masters have all left, there's but a
sapling and no tree.

It makes no sense

There's this summer that has no end.
There's a bird down in a hunter's nest.
A cat and a dog all grey and gloom.
There's a sound from and old man's chair,
and I can hear the hunter's haggard breath.
He's cutting wood for this cold autumn's full
moon.
There's another dog by the spring below
and he howl's, meaning there's a storm not far
below the mountain top.

Music

There, where music is born,
Birds soar into the sky unbound.

There, where the music is born,
The Phoenix is reborn.
The ashes fly into the wind
and each and every teardrop,
and all that touches the ground
or the water in that pond,
echoes down to the Netherworld.

All that was, is and will ever be.
Comes from sound.
Everything that had, has or will ever exist,
It all makes a sound.
It sends wave out into the world.

The world comes together as one,
one, into the vast, eternal peace of the Universe.
There, where music is born.

White-blue light

I walk along the cold stone path.
There is a white-blue light,
and then I follow with right trust.
It is white and not that fast.
It's not dark blue, it can't be but true.

We walk down three flights of stairs.
Now there's the light and one long path,
It may be just me, but I feel like I'm not me.

I've now forgot and there's no time.
Here's a door and a tall dog.
There're some gates I've now been told.

Now yes, I do recall!
There's a stone-cold bed, where I then lay.
Yes, I do recall!

It was then, all on step ten.
Now there's just a poor pale frame.
So now I'm cold and was on last breath,
with but this chance, I step tonight
and then I walk like a white-blue light.

Kiss

I light an incense for the days past
and a candle for those to come.
I raise a glass for those still left,
I take a bow for those long gone.
I kiss you one, to see it twice.
I kiss you thrice to see the vice.

Moon

I look at you when the time is right.
I pray for you to the cold, white Moon.
I sing and I sing and it's all for naught.
You are my music!
And infinite and vast are you.
A hundred thousand flowers all in bloom.
My heart is pierced,
And oh, I so wish but for one kiss.
My time is gone and I shall leave,
All I want is to see you now.
Let die, but let me die in piece.
Only in your arms can I die now, so I go there,
Behind the trees.
Where there's a garden filled with flowers.
The flowers with your name
So I may die in your embrace.